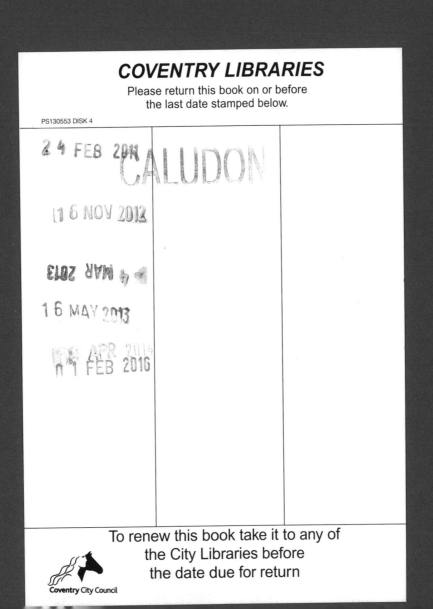

EXTREME MACHINES

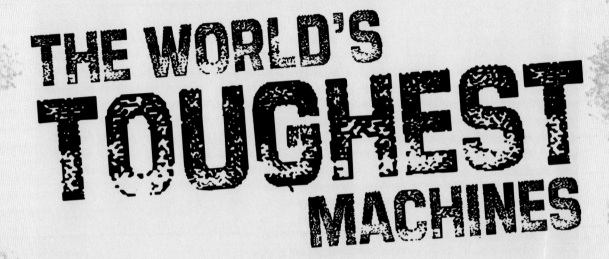

THE WORLD'S TOUGHEST MACHINES

Judy Kentor Schmauss

www.raintreepublishers.co.uk
Visit our website to find out
more information about
Raintree books.

To order:

☎ Phone 0845 6044371

🖨 Fax +44 (0) 1865 312263

💻 Email myorders@raintreepublishers.co.uk

Customers from outside the UK please telephone +44 1865 312262

Raintree is an imprint of Capstone Global Library
Limited, a company incorporated in England and
Wales having its registered office at 7 Pilgrim Street,
London, EC4V 6LB – Registered company number:
6695582

Text © Capstone Global Library Limited 2011
First published in hardback in 2011
The moral rights of the proprietor have been asserted.

Edited by Nancy Dickmann and Megan Cotugno
Designed by Jo Hinton-Malivoire
Picture research by Tracy Cummins
Originated by Capstone Global Library
Printed and bound in China by CTPS

ISBN 978 1 406216 90 5 (hardback)
15 14 13 12 11
10 9 8 7 6 5 4 3 2 1

British Library Cataloguing in Publication Data
Schmauss, Judy Kentor.
The world's toughest machines. -- (Extreme machines)
629'.046-dc22
A full catalogue record for this book is available from
the British Library.

Acknowledgments
We would like to thank the following for permission
to reproduce photographs: Alamy p. **4** (Tony DiZinno
/ TRANSTOCK); BAE Systems pp. **8**, **9**; Corbis pp.
7 (© Transtock), **20** (© Juan Carlos Ulate/Reuters),
21 (© Duomo), **27** bottom (© Jim Reed), **21** top
(© Gene Blevins/LA Daily News); DefenseImagery.
com p. **18** (ROBERT K GYSGT BLANKENSHIP, USMC);
Getty Images pp. **12** (SSPL), **13** (David McNew),
14 (CORTEZ/AFP), **15** (Car Culture), **19** (JEWEL
SAMAD/AFP), **23** (Pierre Mion/National Geographic),
26 (Carsten Peter); istockphoto p. **5** (© Don Bayley);
NASA p. **24** (JPL); NOAA Photo Library p. **22** (OAR/
National Undersea Research Program (NURP));
Photo Researchers, Inc. p. **25** (Atlas Photo Bank);
Shutterstock pp. **6** (Stephen Mcsweeny), **10** (Alexey
Fateev), **11** (Frontpage); U.S. Marine Corps photo pp.
16 (Sgt. Jason W. Fudge), **17**.

Cover photograph of US 2nd Infantry Division M-1A1
Abraham tanks reproduced with permission of Getty
Images (AFP).

Every effort has been made to contact copyright
holders of any material reproduced in this book. Any
omissions will be rectified in subsequent printings if
notice is given to the publisher.

Disclaimer
All the Internet addresses (URLs) given in this book
were valid at the time of going to press. However, due
to the dynamic nature of the Internet, some addresses
may have changed, or sites may have changed or
ceased to exist since publication. While the author and
Publishers regret any inconvenience this may cause
readers, no responsibility for any such changes can be
accepted by either the author or the Publishers.

Some words are shown in bold, **like this**. You can find
out what they mean by looking in the glossary.

Contents

Tough machines 4

Move that dirt! 6

One tough vehicle. 8

Dig it! 10

Through the earth 12

A safe ride 14

Mine-resistant trucks 16

A mighty tank 18

It's a monster!. .20

Down in the sea. 22

Out in space 24

Into the tornado 26

Test yourself!. 28

Glossary. 30

Find out more 31

Index 32

Tough machines

There are many types of machine. Some of them need tender, loving care. Their drivers keep them inside so they don't get scratched. Other machines are tougher than that. They do some of the world's hardest jobs!

Nobody polishes this machine!

Move that dirt!

If you need to move a lot of dirt, a **bulldozer** is the machine to use. Its curved blade easily pushes soil, rocks, and anything else out of the way. A powerful engine keeps it moving forward.

blade

EXTREME FACT

Some bulldozers can weigh over 90 tonnes!

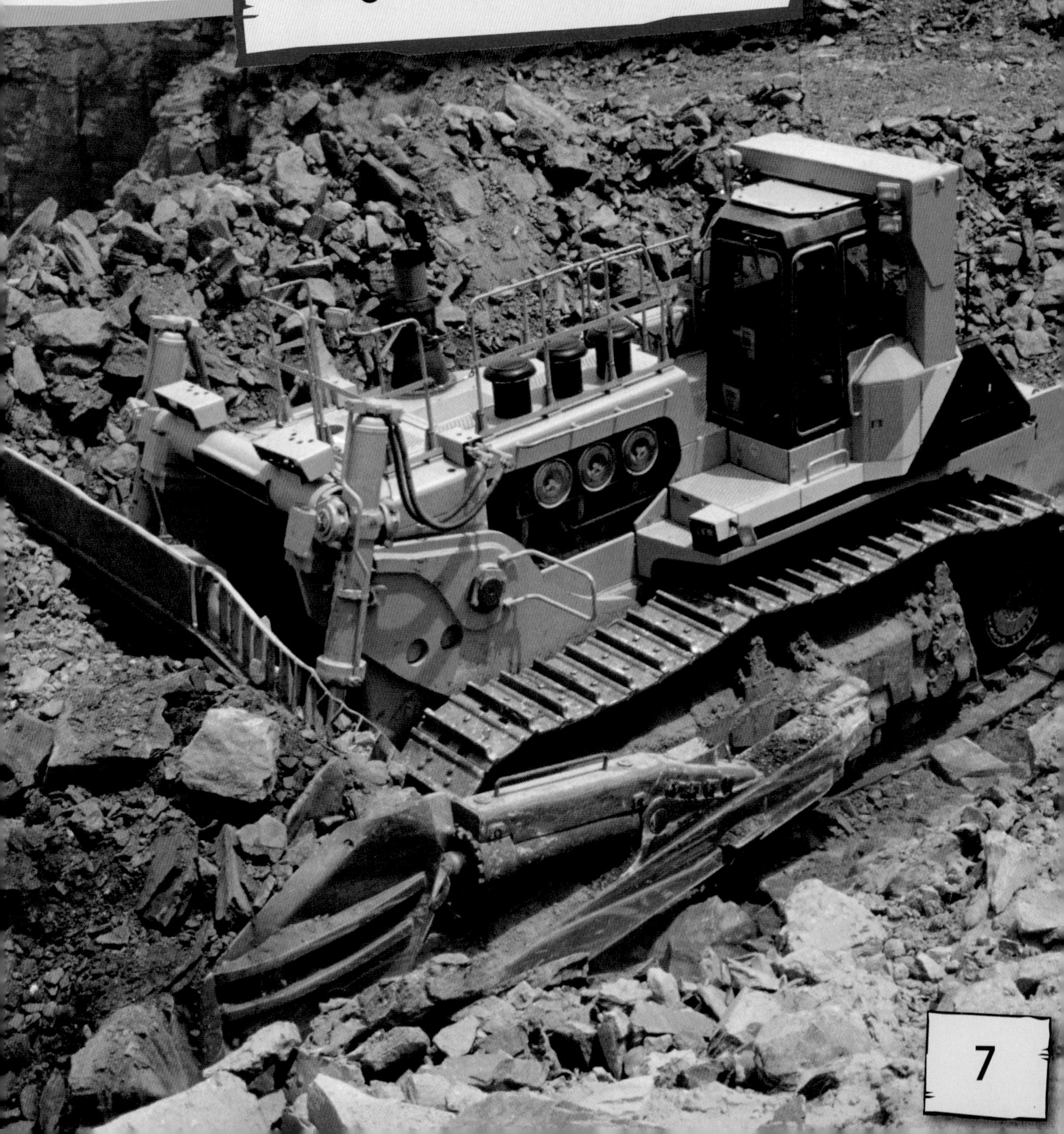

One tough vehicle

The Terrier is an armoured military vehicle. It weighs about 27 tonnes! On the front of the Terrier is a huge bucket. This bucket is used to move obstacles that get in the way.

EXTREME FACT

The Terrier can be operated by remote control. It also has night vision so it can see in the dark!

Dig it!

Excavators do all types of job. Some use their buckets to dig up dirt. This one is knocking down a house! Excavators smash through wood, rocks, and whatever else gets in their way.

buckets

This excavator has many buckets to scoop up dirt more quickly.

Through the earth

This fierce machine is used to dig tunnels. Known as a **mole**, its front end has big steel teeth built into it. The front end spins around and around. The steel teeth cut through soil and rocks. The soil and rocks are carried out of the back by a **conveyor belt**.

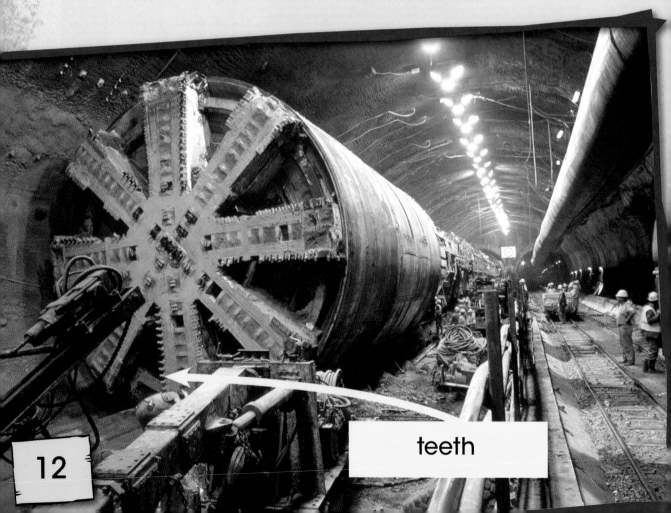

teeth

A safe ride

This is a very tough car. Its tyres can move even if they're flat. If a bullet hits the petrol tank, it doesn't blow up. And the windows are bullet **resistant**. A bullet might scratch it, but it won't get through.

EXTREME FACT

What makes windows bullet resistant? A special material is put between two pieces of glass. The material helps **absorb**, or take in, a bullet's energy and stops it.

Mine-resistant trucks

In war zones, there is danger everywhere. A tough machine is needed to keep soldiers safe. This Cougar can take almost anything. A blast-proof body protects drivers from exploding mines in the ground.

bullet-**resistant** glass

A mighty tank

The armour on the M1A1 Abrams tank is so tough that rockets bounce off it. That's because the armour is made from a type of metal that is stronger than steel.

EXTREME FACT

This tank's guns can shoot a target more than a mile away!

It's a monster!

Bigfoot. Gravedigger. These names sound like monsters. They are monsters all right - monster trucks! Monster trucks race each other over ramps and rows of cars. They crush anything that gets in their way.

Down in the sea

Some tough machines go to extreme places. *Alvin*, a **submersible,** or underwater machine, takes scientists to the bottom of the sea. The weight of the water would crush other vehicles. But *Alvin* is made of strong **titanium**.

Alvin found the wreck of the RMS *Titanic*.

Alvin

RMS *Titanic*

Out in space

Voyager 1 was sent into space in 1977. It explores our solar system. *Voyager 1* can stand up to **solar winds** that blow at up to 3.2 million kph (2 million mph). *Voyager 1* might keep going for another 20 to 30 years!

EXTREME FACT
A disk on board holds greetings to aliens in 55 different languages!

Into the tornado

This machine drives straight into tornadoes. It is covered with armour like a tank to stop it blowing away. But this machine is faster than a tank. It can catch up with a tornado—and take pictures inside it!

tornado

This machine needs to be faster and tougher than a tornado!

Test yourself!

Try to match each question to the correct answer.

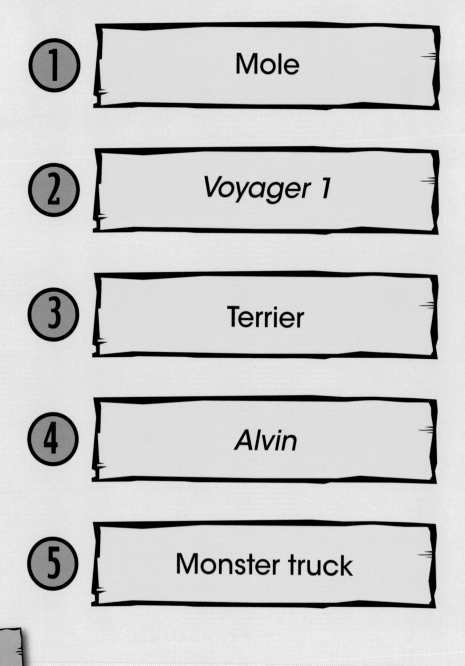

① Mole

② *Voyager 1*

③ Terrier

④ *Alvin*

⑤ Monster truck

Answers:
1 = e, 2 = b, 3 = a, 4 = d, 5 = c

e Which machine digs tunnels?

d Which machine takes scientists to the bottom of the ocean floor?

c Which machine goes over rows of cars?

b Which machine tells us about what's out in space?

a Which tough vehicle has night vision?

Glossary

absorb to soak up like a sponge soaks up water

bulldozer a large truck used for pushing things

conveyor belt a moving surface that carries things along

mole a machine that digs holes

resistant to hold up without breaking against the force or effect of something

submersible a vehicle that can go below the surface of the water

solar winds winds in space caused by the Sun

titanium a strong metal

Find out more

Books

Construction Vehicles, Terry Jennings
(Saunders Book Company, 2009)

Trucks: Pickups to Big Rigs, Adrianna Morganelli
(Crabtree Publishing Company, 2007)

Websites

Everything about JCB construction machines
http://www.jcbexplore.com/
Find out how JCB excavators and other machines work.

Monster trucks
http://www.monstertrucks.net/
This website answers many questions about monster
trucks.

Voyager 1 and *2*
**www.worsleyschool.net/science/files/extreme/
machines.html**
Follow the travels of *Voyager 1* and *2* through the
solar system.

More on tanks
http://www.tankmuseum.org/
Visit the tank museum website to find out about different
types of tank.

Find out

How big can a
bulldozer be?

Index

aliens 25
Alvin submersible 22, 23
armour 18, 26

Bigfoot monster truck 20
blades 6
buckets 10, 11
bulldozers 6, 7
bullet-resistant glass 14, 15,
   17

conveyor belts 12
Cougar truck 16

engines 6, 8
excavators 10, 11

Gravedigger monster
   truck 20
guns 19

M1A1 Abrams tank 18,
   19
mines 16
moles 12
monster trucks 20

rockets 18

spacecraft 24, 25
submersibles 22, 23

tanks 18, 19, 26
teeth 12
Terrier 8, 9
titanium 22
tornadoes 26
trucks 16
tunnels 12
tyres 14

Voyager 1 spacecraft
   24, 25

war 16
windows 14, 15